# Prokofiev

**Wendy Lynch**

Heinemann Library
Chicago, Illinois

© 2000 Reed Educational & Professional Publishing
Published by Heinemann Library,
an imprint of Reed Educational & Professional Publishing,
Chicago, IL
Customer Service  888-454-2279

Visit our website at www.heinemannlibrary.com

Designed by Visual Image
Illustrations by Shirley Bellwood
Originated by Dot Gradations
Printed and bound in Hong Kong/China

04 03 02
10 9 8 7 6 5 4 3 2

**Library of Congress Cataloging-in-Publication Data**

Lynch, Wendy, 1945-
    Prokofiev / Wendy Lynch.
       p. cm. – (Lives and times)
    Includes bibliographical references (p.   ) and index.
    Summary: An introductory biography of the composer of such works
    as "Peter and the Wolf" and "The Love for Three Oranges."
    ISBN 1-57572-220-8 (library binding)
    1. Prokofiev, Sergey, 1891-1953 Juvenile literature.
    2. Composers—Soviet Union Biography Juvenile literature.
    [1. Prokofiev, Sergey, 1891-1953. 2. Composers.] I. Title.
    II. Series: Lives and times (Des Plaines, Ill.)
    ML3930.P77L96  2000
    780'.92—dc21
       [B]                                                    99-37331
                                                                 CIP

**Acknowledgments**

The Publishers would like to thank the following for permission to reproduce photographs: AKG London, pp 17, 23; Haddon Davies, pp. 20, 21; Novosti (London), pp. 15, 16, 22, 23 (inset); Prokofiev Archive, p. 19.

Cover photograph reproduced with permission of AKG London.

Every effort has been made to contact copyright holders of any material reproduced in this book. Any omissions will be rectified in subsequent printings if notice is given to the publisher.

Some words are shown in bold, **like this.** You can find out what they mean by looking in the glossary.

# Contents

# Part One

Sergei Prokofiev was born in Sontsovka, Russia, on April 23, 1891. At night, before he went to bed, he loved to listen to his mother playing the piano.

When Prokofiev was five years old, his
mother taught him how to play the piano.
He also began to make up his own music.
This is called **composing**.

By 1904, Prokofiev had written a **symphony**, four **operas,** and many pieces of music for the piano. He also loved to play **chess** with his father.

When he was twelve, Prokofiev went to study music in St. Petersburg, Russia. It was difficult for him to make friends because all the other students were much older than he was.

Prokofiev had many new ideas about music. He worked hard at **composing**. People did not always like his music, because it sounded strange to them. But in 1914, he won a competition playing his own music.

Prokofiev traveled in Europe and the United States. In New York, he wrote an **opera** called *The Love for Three Oranges*. Many people liked it. Prokofiev became famous.

When Prokofiev was 29, he went to live in Paris. Here, he married a woman named Lina, and they had two sons. Prokofiev's mother also came to live with them.

In 1927, Prokofiev went on a **tour** of Russia to play his music. His tour was very successful. This made Prokofiev feel homesick. In 1936, he and his family went to live in Russia.

Prokofiev wanted to help children learn
the different musical instruments in an
**orchestra**. So in 1936 he wrote music to
go with a popular Russian story about
a boy named Peter. It was called *Peter
and the Wolf*.

The Bird by the flute

The Duck by the oboe

The Cat by the clarinet

The Wolf by the French horn

Every **character** in *Peter and the Wolf* is played by a different instrument. In the story, Peter meets a bird, a duck, a cat, and a wolf!

Prokofiev wrote a **ballet** called *Romeo and Juliet* in 1936. But now it became hard for him to write the kind of music that he wanted. This was because the ruler of Russia did not like Prokofiev's music.

Sergei Prokofiev **composed** music every day of his life, even when he was traveling and there was no piano or desk for him to use. He became ill and died on March 5, 1953.

# Part Two

There are many ways in which we can find out about Sergei Prokofiev. People took many pictures of him. Here is a photo of Prokofiev as a baby with his parents.

Many artists made drawings and paintings of Prokofiev. Here is one that was painted in 1934.

Prokofiev traveled around the world to play his music. This is a poster for a **concert** he played in Spain in 1935. He wrote many letters to his family and friends when he was away from home.

Asociación de Cultura Musical

MADRID

AÑO 15    1935·1936    Concierto 3

SERGE
PROKOFIEFF
PIANISTA

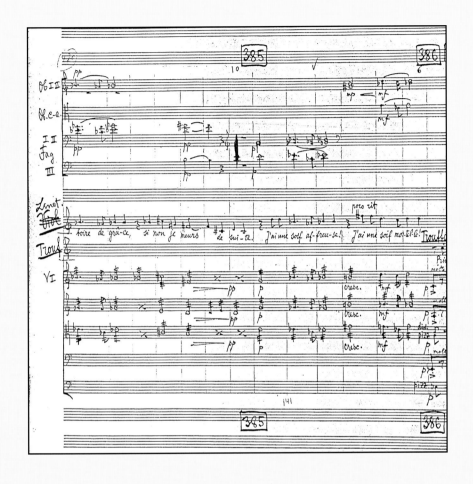

Here is a **manuscript** written by
Prokofiev. It shows how he wrote music
on a page. He wrote some music as a
birthday present for his old music teacher.

There are many ways in which you can hear Prokofiev's music. You can go to a **concert**, or you can listen to a CD, like this one of *Peter and the Wolf*. You can also hear his music on the radio.

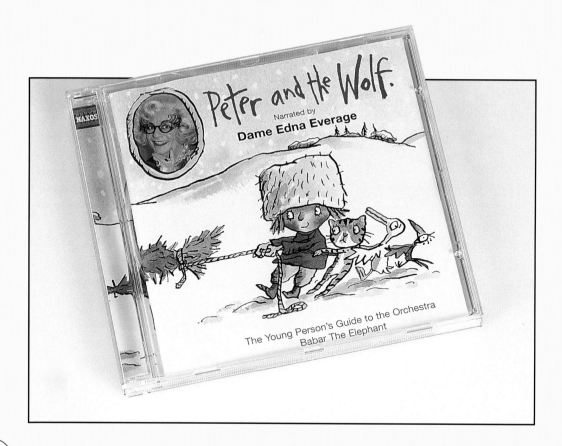

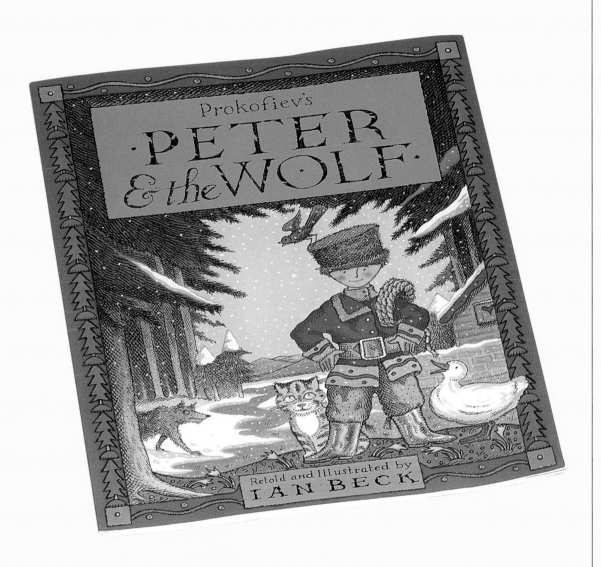

Prokofiev's music is still very popular. This book tells the story of *Peter and the Wolf.*

We can find out many things about Sergei Prokofiev's life and music. This picture shows what some of the costumes looked like for his **opera** *The Love for Three Oranges.*

Prokofiev's wife, Lina, helped to start the Prokofiev **Archive** in London. Here, you can see newspaper stories, films, letters, and books about Prokofiev. These mean that he will always be remembered.

# Glossary

This glossary explains difficult words, and helps you to say words which may be hard to say.

**archive**   place to keep a lot of information. You say *ar-kive*.

**ballet**   dancing and movement that tells a story. You say *bal-ay*.

**character**   person or animal in a story. You say *care-ak-ter*.

**chess**   game played on a checkered board

**compose**   to make up music

**concert**   public show by musicians

**manuscript**   anything written by hand. You say *man-you-script*.

**opera**   play that is sung, not spoken

**orchestra**   large group of musicians who play together. You say *or-kes-tra*.

**symphony**   long piece of music for many musical instruments. You say *sim-fun-ee*.

**tour**   long trip to different countries

# Index

# More Books to Read

Eastman, David. *Peter & the Wolf.* Mahwah, N.J.: Troll Communications, 1988.

Kendall, Catherine W. *Stories of Composers for Young Musicians.* Takoma Park, Md.: Toadwood Publishers, 1982.